A LADDER OF CRANES

a ladder of cranes

Tom Sexton

University of Alaska Press | Fairbanks

University of Alaska Press
P.O. Box 756240
Fairbanks, AK 99775-6240

Library of Congress Cataloging-in-Publication Data
Sexton, Tom, 1940-
[Poems. Selections]
A ladder of cranes / Tom Sexton.
pages ; cm
ISBN 978-1-60223-257-0 (pbk. : alk. paper) —
ISBN 978-1-60223-258-7 (electronic)
I. Title.
PS3569.E88635A6 2015
811'.54—dc23
        2014023212

Book and cover design by Kristina Kachele Design, llc
Cover photo by John R. DeLapp, Alaska Stock

This publication was printed on acid-free paper that meets the
minimum requirements for ANSI / NISO Z39.48–1992 (R2002)
(Permanence of Paper for Printed Library Materials).

For Sharyn

I am grateful to the editors of the following publications where a few of these poems have appeared: *Assisi, The Alaska Star, The Aurorean, Cirque, Ice Floe, Parnassus, Salamander,* and *The Christian Science Monitor.*

Contents

A LADDER OF CRANES

The Bird Walkers of Roosevelt Park

Thin as cigarettes held between stained
fingers, they appear around dawn,

old men walking to this park from small
rooms and tenements in Chinatown,

gripping covered cages, whispering,
fearful of waking their sleeping birds.

When the air begins to warm, cages
are uncovered and songs rise, slowly

at first, like mist rising from a millet field.
The old men nod, chirp like crickets.

Pied-billed Grebe on the Concord River

I look at it three times before my eyes
admit it's there in an eddy
where a canal flows into the river
below a breached sucker-hoarding dam.
Now river herring return in the spring.

Only its cane-handle-smooth head
is above the water before it dives.
If I stand here in the rain much longer,
I'll turn to water and then to herring-
milt, to cosmic spawn. Imagine that.

At the Fruitlands Museum, Harvard, Massachusetts

Today I saw Bronson Alcott's ghost
wearing a frock coat made of snow

in this orchard that was part of his farm
not far from New Hampshire's lingering dark.

He held a walking stick made of light
and it seemed that he would soon take flight.

Emerson, shepherd to the Transcendental flock,
slipped river stones into Alcott's pockets

to keep his friend from drifting away
when they walked here at the break of day.

A dreamer, perhaps even a fool, he believed
that man could blossom like an apple tree.

Blueberry Barren at Dusk

Wind has stripped it of snow
leaving a rocky field that glows

like embers beneath ash, a darker
mood, an open wound, late March

even the north wind seems to sigh,
not even a single crow in the sky.

From the idling car, I watch it darken.
Above tall pines to the east a single star.

Eastport, Maine

The afternoon sky is no longer crow-black
when I walk, I can see Indian Island at 4 p.m.
Beyond two cormorants skimming the water,
gulls cover a rock that will soon disappear.
Light seems to seep from their feathers.
A dragger, lights on, heads for the breakwater.
Over Campobello Island, moon rising, scallop-white.

Star Marrow

Last night, I read that everything contains
traces of ancient stars: snails climbing
a moss-covered rock as if it were a mountain,
the rock, lichen on the bark of a tree,
the sudden luminescence of an opening shell,
a vein of ore at the bottom of a shaft,
baleen in the mouth of a breaching whale,
the cloak the ocean wears on a clear night,
me writing these lines by the window.
We have star marrow in our bones, star marrow.

First Anna's Hummingbird
Sighted in Newfoundland

"At first I thought it was a glint off the taillight
of a car on the road that runs along the bay.
It was dusk and I was about to make our tea,"
the older sister who was first to see it told
the reporter. "Then in the morning we saw
it at a feeder we'd forgotten to put away,"
the younger sister said. "It wore a bright red toque
and the greenest jumper that we've ever seen."
"If we believed in the little people, I'd say it was
one of them," the first sister said, "but we don't
and they're not seen until November anyway."

Statue of a Union Soldier

It seems to be almost alive at twilight
this bronze statue of a Union soldier
ramrod straight on the littered common
of a small town where only the elderly
walk to the white-framed church on Sunday,
a church that survives on rummage sales,
selling old clothes and stacks of used
canning jars that glow like fireflies then fade.
Were there shad blossoms on the banks
of the pond below the now-abandoned mill
when his company marched off to war?
An orb spider has spun a web between
the bayonet on his rifle and his shoulder.

A Ladder of Cranes

On a Sunday afternoon west of Winnipeg
without a truck on our tail for mile after mile,

past fields still covered with melted snow,
beneath a sky so clear it's about to disappear

while we listen to a soprano singing
Schubert's *Ave Maria* on the car's radio,

a ladder of cranes lifting, moving away
over a windbreak with almost visible leaves.

White-tailed Buck in a Pasture

Beneath a tree with moon-yellow apples
still on its branches in late November,
a small buck is making a circle in new snow.
"They're only pig apples," a real estate agent
told me when asked. "Good for nothing else."
The buck pauses, bends its head to the snow,
then looks up at the branches as if it's waiting
for another miraculous moon-yellow apple to fall.

Winter Thaw

Mist drifts over tangled blackberry canes
over saplings wind has hooped to the ground,

it drifts past a cup-shaped songbird's nest
that's anchored to an eye-level branch,

a nest that's made of grass and hair,
it climbs a tamarack's knotty vertebrae

then like a magician's coin it disappears
leaving behind a voice that seems to say:

"Once I was a vernal pool, once I was a glacier.
Step out of those winter-weary bones and rise."

Glass Eels

Caught in a net placed in the river
at dusk when the tide was rising,

eels clear as glass but for their eyes
and the faintest trace of their spines,

eels that will never darken in a pond
or return to the Sargasso Sea to spawn,

eels that gather light from the stars
as if one depends upon the other.

Someone will come by to empty the net
spilling them, but not yet, not yet.

Po Chü-I's Cook

After a daylong struggle with a poem
that had left him needing a drink, Po Chü-I
would chant it to his family's cook,

the illiterate cook who legend tells us
saw a tortoise on the bottom of a lake
where others saw their own reflection.

If she frowned while he chanted,
Po Chü-I retreated to his study.
Stars appeared. His door stayed closed.

The sun climbed. The air warmed.
The ice on his cup melted to a pupil.
The cook appeared carrying leeks.

Mozart's Starling

If, while sitting on the maestro's shoulder
while he composed, it spied
a murmuration of other starlings
moving across the sky like a quill
it whispered "*das war schon*" in Mozart's ear.

When it died too young, a grieving Mozart
wrote a poem to be read at its funeral.
All the mourners, those inside the church
and those on its spire, wore black.
Above the church, one star was noted.

On the Death of Seamus Heaney

He is crossing those four green fields now.
On the horizon, blossoms falling like snow.
A chorus calls his name. He does not break stride
toward a small house. He can hear his mother's sigh.
Now he eyes his father holding a tall ladder
and at the top of the ladder stands his brother
skimming the gable, shaping the letters *S.H.*
in wet plaster. It covers his hands and knees
as blood did on the day he died. They turn
to go inside where his mother is churning butter.

Innisfree, Western Alberta

I imagine a woman staring at the frozen
landscape of Alberta from the narrow window
of a house just big enough to hold two
souls in harness, that and little more.
When the wind rises again, ghosts will knock
on the door, but she will not be frightened
the way she was the winter she arrived
from the east to marry a man she didn't know.
Her sister in Ontario sent a poem by William
Butler Yeats about an island in an Irish lake.
She'd written "another Innisfree" on the back.
"A dreamer's poem" her husband snarled
when he found her reading it at the table.
"Bee-loud glade, was the fool ever stung?"
When spring comes she'll row to the island in
Birch Lake and read the poem to her favorite tree,
the white birch her husband promised to cut down,
then she'll help him choose a lamb to slaughter.

Mundare, Alberta

Our dog-eared travel guide invited us to see
the town's renowned Ukrainian monastery
and the world's largest statue of a sausage
by Stawnichy's meat processing plant
that's a short walk from the blue buffalo.
We'd already seen the world's largest
Easter egg that morning at Vegreville.
The monastery could wait. We were hungry
so we headed for the only café in sight.

All heads turned to watch us when we sat
at the only table that seemed to be empty.
The farmers watching us appeared to be carved
from wood. Only the waitress spoke and all
she said was "soup's borsht." Through a crack
in the kitchen's door, we saw what appeared
to be a molten kettle attached to a glowing cable.
When she came back, she put two steaming
bowls on the table. "Eat," she said, "you can taste
the earth." We drained our bowls. Asked for more.

The Wolf of Gubbio

When he was too lame to wander the streets
of Gubbio begging for alms to give the poor
the way he had seen his brother Francis doing
when they met on the road that fateful morning,
the morning Francis spoke to him with kindness,
he rode in a cart pulled by two sheep that brother
Ugilino made for him to take him from door to door,
and no matter how poor the villagers were they
always saved a few scraps of food for their wolf
who was not evil but starving when he terrorized
the village, and he saved a few scraps for the mice.

Gray Wolf

To write a poem about a gray wolf
it is best to have seen one hunting
beneath a hornet's nest of dark
cloud along the edge of a marsh
still mottled with winter's last snow
to remember the angle of its head
and the blade-thin length of its body
as it takes your measure, disappears.

Medieval Bestiary: The Wolf

If a wolf steps on a branch and it makes a noise,
the wolf will chew its offending foot to a stub.

If a wolf sees a man before the man sees the wolf,
the man will lose his voice for a year.

If you pluck the tuft of hair at the end of a wolf's tail,
you can use it as a love potion as long as the wolf is alive.

If a wolf sees a woman who is about to give birth,
the child will be born with long, pointy teeth.

If you see a wolf's eyes shining like lamps at night,
it might be the devil hunting and not a wolf at all.

Killing the Kenai Peninsula's Wolves

Ripe blueberries heavy on their stems
by the side of the trail where I go
to pick. They're icy cold. Beyond them,
rolling hills below peaks waiting for snow.
When my bucket's full, my hands are icy cold.
What will I do if I meet a wolf leaving its cover?
I saw one hunting a moose calf years ago.
Was Saint Francis a fool to call a wolf brother?

Miners almost killed them off with strychnine.
Bureaucrats now say that they must go.
After deep snow, they'll shoot them from the air.
I think of Heaney's poem about the last Irish
wolf. It was shot by a Quaker centuries ago.
Distant swans. Ice will form on ponds tonight.

Fall Raspberries

On the raspberry canes, last night's icy
rain and the last berries, smaller now
but sweeter. Near the fence, a faint yellow
haze of leaves in the early morning light.

Even though my hands are stiff from cold,
I pick every single berry I can reach.
Magpies do a little dance, call me a thief.
The canes will soon be buried under snow.

Fireweed

Fireweed seeds in a light breeze above a narrowing dirt road,
long white beards catching the slanting morning light
in the Old Believer village of Nikolaevsk, drifting past
a domed church with ikons painted on its wooden doors,
floating over fading meadows toward the Caribou Hills,
patriarchs about to settle down for a long winter under snow.

Insomnia

Sleepless, I watch our birch trees glowing
even though it's only 3 a.m. Not a sound
is coming from the snow-covered road.
How can snow be like light coming down?

This must be how angels once appeared
to the willing, their great wings silent,
filling the room with otherworldly light,
taking their hands, whispering, "Have no fear."

To the Chinese Poets

Old masters, I swore to leave you at peace
to not lean on you in my verse again,

but it's you I hear in the wind as we climb
toward the summit of a mountain pass

where we hope to find a room for the night.
At the plowed edge of the road, the stiff

bodies of songbirds, feathered migrants
who never reached their destination.

The buds on the trees are covered with ice.
Tell me again of blossoms drifting down.

Black Spruce

Outside the cabin's window, the November
snow is so deep it seems Li Bai's frenzied
Immortals have left the safety of his poems
to grind all the clouds in the world to a fine
powder that they're dumping on the marsh,
burying the black spruce, even the tallest.
When spring comes, the spruce will reappear
tilting in every direction, unsteady revelers,
green jackets glistening, wearing halos of pollen
while the last of the snow at their feet disappears.

Fall Migration

At dawn, the lake's covered with thin
ice around the island where friends have a cabin.
Their young daughter's raincoat's on a hook
above her boots and a stack of coloring books.

There's enough misery in the world to fill
the lake with tears, enough to make it spill
my thoughts while I watch a yellow warbler
on a twig flare like a match then disappear.

To reach the lake just now, it must have flown
all night over tall peaks covered with snow.
I feel a stirring, a faint hope, in my heart
that our journey is also out of the dark.

To the Poet John Haines on His Eighty-fifth Birthday

It was almost too cold to walk today
but I knew it was the perfect weather
to see the mountains to the north,
part of the range I've seen from your cabin.
As I walked, I thought of your recent letter:
a touch of pneumonia, nothing more,
you wrote. I'll be working again before long.

Can you see the mountains from where
you write or the wide palm of your river?
Do you sit by a window in your old sweater
still redolent of green alder and smoke?
I watch you harrumph then begin to write —
measuring each word, holding it to the light
until the stars appear, your owl takes flight.

Resolution Park

Anchorage, Alaska

With his back turned to the city of Anchorage
that honors him with this park and statue,
Captain Cook looks out on Turnagain Arm
where his quest for the Northwest Passage
came to its end. His flagship, in miniature,
sails on in filtered air above the dealmakers,
conventioneers, and tourists who linger
in the lobby of the Hotel Captain Cook.
He cannot see the "fuck for god" someone carved
beneath his pedestal, nor can he see "love
takes persperpence" written with a magic marker.
Cook's gaze is fixed upon the silty rising tide.
Cell phone in hand, a man is telling his lover
in Hawaii about the mahi-mahi he had for dinner.

The Man from Here

Pale green leaves were opening on the trees
when I saw him climbing the bank from a beach
that appears when Cook Inlet's tide is slack.
Smoke rose from the embers of his driftwood fire.
Once on the trail, he began to walk toward me
as an ancestor of his must have walked toward
Captain Cook's crew sent out to see if this inlet
was their goal: the fabled Northwest Passage.
A street person and he's after change, I thought,
but all he wanted was to know where I was from.
"Massachusetts," I said, "been here over fifty years."
He swept his arm in an arc from Point Possession
named by Cook to the mountains in every direction
before he smiled at me and said, "I'm from here."

Galaxies

for Dana Wilde

On a ridge beneath a northern sky that's
just dark enough for me to see the stars
at midnight, I come upon star flowers,
a triad of sevens: sepals, petals, leaves,
flowing yellow-white like the Milky Way
toward a weedy pond, an earthbound
galaxy that lifts my mood and humbles me.
One light years away, the other underfoot.

The Church at Ninilchik, Alaska

for Will and Mina Jacobs

Three decades ago, I held a crown of gold
over the veiled head of a young bride
in this small Orthodox church near the road.
It seemed to float in the afternoon sky
above the slate-green inlet. "Let it touch her
hair and their marriage will certainly fail,"
an old woman whispered in my ear.
Superstition? Their marriage melted like hail.

When I see the church today, will the priest
be climbing the muddy path from the village,
a small man with slightly Asiatic features
so full of his faith it overflowed, spilled?
His shoes were dark roots pulled from the ground
when he arrived. Light rain was coming down.

Swans on Cook Inlet

After an early October storm, I watch a pair
of swans forced to take shelter on the inlet.
I'm late for supper, but I linger on the trail
remembering when my marriage was on thin
ice. I had left two of our tent pegs behind
and called my wife's offered blueberries bitter.
I was angry. Our camp stove wouldn't stay lit.
"Half a continent from home," she sighed.

When a swan appeared in the darkening sky,
she said it was the Swan Maiden returning
to her father's house. Our stove sputtered, died,
but I managed to keep our wet fire burning.
Her eyelids and hair were white with frost by dawn.
The tide's rising. The inlet swans will soon move on.

Solitude

December now and I'm reading John Clare's
poems by candlelight, John Clare who knelt
beside the evening primrose and wandered
heath and fen with Solitude for company
to hear the nightingale who lived on song
before his world was measured and enclosed.
My small cabin is far from that lost world
in a place that was wilderness not long ago.
I blow my candle out and go to the window.
Headlights are moving on Chulitna Butte
where ptarmigan once burrowed into snow.

After Walking in Rain on a Sunday Morning

First the waterproof coat that's wetter
than the dog comes off and after it
my favorite Sunday shirt that's stained
my undershirt, then my soggy cords
and jockey shorts. It's a miracle that my
socks are only damp. Almost as naked
as the day I was born but more wrinkled,
I can feel what seem to be pinfeathers
on my arms and shoulders as if this
is a baptism and I'll soon be flying with
the cranes I saw on the mud flats, wings
rising and falling, doffing my red cap as we go.

Reading Li Bai While the Moon Rises

Looking up from the page, I can see
the moon over the snow-dusted

mountains to the east of the city.
It's as round as a coin and golden.

In the background, a voice on
the radio is saying without emotion,

"The Yangtze River dolphin is no more."
I follow Li Bai along the river's bank.

A little unsteady from drinking wine,
He calls, "Princess Baiji, Princess Baiji,"

and a shy dolphin comes to the surface.
Their moon is white and round as a pearl.

The flat voice on the radio says again,
"The Yangtze River dolphin is no more."

Magpie at Twilight

I watch a magpie walking back and forth
in a puddle that will be frozen by morning.
It pauses to adjust its long iridescent tail.
Three ravens are watching from a cable wire.
They seem to know when it's best to keep quiet.
The magpie turns its head for a better look
at me, beakless, shivering in my down jacket.
"Noah sent me out with the dove," it chatters
before it turns away, falls silent for a moment.
The ravens tilt their heads, chortle in disbelief.

Looking at the Ferry Museum's Salish Baskets

In Memory of Jim Petit

And suddenly I'm thinking of that cone of light
that Saa Maa, your Master, helped you shape.
Did you ascend without as much as a sigh
or longing to be here for another day?
I prayed that you'd find a marrow donor.
"We have eight bodies and only one is flesh,"
you said, "feel no sadness when I'm gone.
I'll soon be a Master, this tired body at rest."
You were always amused by my skepticism
of your quest. Like your grandmother who twined
your Salish basket, nature is my prism:
alpenglow, bear grass, cedar, spawning tides.
Last night's frost that layered grass like pollen
glistened at dawn as if the stars had fallen.

Starring, Western Alaska

Orthodox Christmas, the faithful, young and old,
walking from house to house singing in Yup'ik
and Slavonic, their breath visible in the air.

The stars seem to have bent closer to earth
to observe their journey. An elder spins
a wooden star with the Virgin at its center,

a reminder of the star the Wise Men followed.
A child ringing a bell is leading them.
When a star enters a house, it is blessed.

The Loon at Shackford Head

In a cove below where I stand
the ghost of sea smoke
beneath a pale sky, ice underfoot,
then I see the loon, a petroglyph
at first, before it faces north
and I can see its foreneck
a pillar of the purest salt before
it fills the bay with a single glacial call.

Cow Moose and Magpie

A cow moose is eating the new buds
on the birch trees in our yard

while a magpie strolls back and forth
on its back from rump to neck

just to see how it feels to make
the earth tremble when it walks.

They pass my window heading west
toward my neighbor's tulip bed.

Cloudberry Wine

Cloudberries must be ripening in the marsh
that we crossed to reach our small cabin.
Small yellow moons with halos of red
that the Scandinavians call liquid gold.
Every year we picked enough to make wine,
but we were visitors there my wife and I
not hardy enough to put down roots
or solitary enough to consult the stars.
Bundled like monks on the winter solstice,
we filled our glasses, raised them to the marsh.

Our Hand-carved Ornament
of a Great Blue Heron

I watch you lift it from our tree, still redolent
when touched, to put it away for another year:
our great blue heron, my favorite ornament.
Another shot of Newfoundland rum is near
my chair, a nip for my heart. I'm feeling old;
but, when your hands cradle it like a nest,
our first heron rises from its marsh. I hold
my breath. Newly married we're driving north
for the first time again. The aim of all art,
I pontificate, is to lead us toward the light
even when the artist's eye is cold or dark
like the bitter taste of rum however slight.
You tell me I'm more than tipsy and wonder
if it thinks the stars are herons in flight.

President Harding's Pullman Car, Fairbanks, Alaska

Scandal followed him into the ground
like the lover he hid in the closet one night.
It stood beside him when he drove the Golden Spike
at Nenana. Powder flashed. His body swayed.
He had left Washington hoping to get away.
At a Fairbanks paper, he set two lines of type.
Those who watched thought they heard him sigh.
Sleepless, the car swaying, he watched the stars fade.

Now tourists examine his slowly rusting car,
glance up at the sky through stained glass windows.
Someone says, "He looks an awful lot like Bush
and did you see that classy private bar?"
A few scan the offered pamphlets before they go.
Children whine, head for the door in a rush.

Westchester Lagoon

Late May and spring has finally reached
the lagoon. On its far eastern edge
the first calla lily will emerge before long
to stand like a boy at his first dance
with a white handkerchief carefully folded
in the pocket of his shiny new green jacket,
a boy dreaming of gliding across dark water
with a stalk of ripening berries in his hand.

The Mist Net

Even though you're not at my side
when I enter mist from a lake
flowing across a narrow path
like the net we saw an ornithologist
stretching between alders so he
could catch and band songbirds,
I imagine a hand reaching out to lift
you from the mesh because you're
a finer specimen before it untangles
me, feet first, a small drop of water
at the end of my astonished beak.
I'm too common to note or measure,
so I'm quickly released, urged to fly.
You're held for what seems to be forever.
I'll be home before long, before morning.

Reading Housman's "Loveliest of trees, the cherry now"

I look outside and see it snowing
at the end of April, light snow
blossoming on branches still bare
at midnight when the sky was clear

and think of his woodland cherry trees,
how their snowy blossoms eased
his ache for beauty in this world.
The wind picks up. The blossoms swirl.

My book of his poems put aside,
I walk with him at Eastertide
to see the cherry trees in bloom
in light spun on the season's loom.

A Needle's Eye

When a needle's eye of blue appeared
in a sky that seemed to be endless cloud

I pulled the car over to the side of the road
and walked to the boggy edge of a pond

where lilies were just beginning to offer
their golden petals to the morning.

Caught in their slow unfolding
I was petal and seed, a drop of mist

rising higher and higher toward the still-
unthreaded eye until I disappeared.

A Little Poem for the Stars

A few stars are spread across the sky
at dusk like dice rolled by an invisible
hand, or by no hand at all. Because
it's fall where I stand, a comet's tail
of red spills across the mountains.
With no moon, it will be dark before long
and the stars will be endless and bright.
This poem, this flicker, is all I can offer.

Alder Catkins

Beside the bike path into town,
spring's first alder catkins

dazzle like the silk stockings
Ben Franklin wore to wow the queen

when he was invited to Versailles,
new male catkins long and narrow

not quite yellow, veined with red,
catkins that will soon begin to fade.

The woody brown female catkins nod.
Is that snuff or pollen floating in the air?

Alder Catkins after Rain

So where are they now those catkins
that yesterday seemed about to pirouette

then float away lighter than air
to celebrate another spring's arrival?

In their place on all the alders,
sullen teens with yellow dreadlocks

almost touching ground, mumbling
"yo, brown bears are our homies, chill."

Poem Written on the Winter Solstice

By noon the day is an ermine darting
from dark to dark, a ripple of light
far to the west a little after four.
On the stove, the earthy scent
of potatoes, carrots, and parsnips
so sweet they stun the tongue.
I dug them from the garden in October.
Turn off your computer, your tablet,
unlock your door and step outside.

On Being Asked to Write a
Poem about the Moon

On a lagoon not far from home, a grebe chick
that two weeks ago was an egg in a floating nest
made of marsh grass and bits of aquatic debris,
is now on the back of its mother who has a small
silver fish in her beak. They'll be here until ice
forms in the shallows by the shore and snow
begins to move down the mountains. Thank you
for asking me to send a poem about the moon,
but I've vowed not to write about it for a year
though it's rising orange as the male grebe's neck.

European Starling

Black-suited maestro dipping his yellow beak
like a quill into a sky that's icy blue
from his perch on our chokecherry tree,
trying his G sharp, then swooping, falling,
tilting his head as if he expects a chorus
of other starlings to appear: a whirlwind
of wings, plume of smoke, over the silt-
heavy inlet toward the Alaska Range, but
he's alone, a solitary, composer and composed.

American Dipper

Like a preacher bending over
his sermon, it bends over the swift
water of a stream that will soon
be locked in thick ice until May.
Its dark coat of dense feathers
ends where you expect to see a tail.
It dips its head three times, dives
then rises quickly to the surface
with a tiny silver fish in its beak.
It swallows, resumes its meditation.

Independence Mine, August

I like to think the miners looked up and
sighed when they emerged from the maze
of endless tunnels and saw the moon
overhead as bright as the gold
they blasted from the unwilling rock,
gold that kept their families from the cold.

I like to think one or two stooped to pick
a handful of berries for their children
while they followed the moon's light down
to the boomtown they once called home,
berries as ripe as the full moon now
spilling its light like honey from a spoon.

The Advent Bear

for Sarah Isto

They had just turned the lights
off and placed an Advent

candle in the window
when it appeared on the street,

a black bear, heavy with fat,
ambling toward their window.

Had the candle drawn it from
the woods at the top of the hill?

It was snowing lightly even
though they could see the stars.

A small constellation of wet flakes
rippled on its massive back.